at last sight

Arni Haraldsson

essay by
Anne Brydon

London Regional Art & Historical Museums
421 Ridout Street North, London, Ontario N6A 5H4

acknowledgements

IN FEBRUARY 1999 I first saw the work of Arni Haraldsson at the Vancouver Art Gallery. Since I am an anthropologist who does research in Iceland and amongst the descendants of Icelandic immigrants to Canada, his distinctly Icelandic name caught my eye. But his elegant, dispassionate photographs of modernist architecture truly captivated me and resonated with my own fascination with urban environments. The idea of a solo exhibit at the LRAHM quickly developed. I had wanted to give something back to the arts community that has been my home since I moved to London in 1994. I also wanted to mark the Icelandic Canadian Millennium Celebrations with an exhibit that links Canada and Iceland through the arts, and draws attention to the architectural features of contemporary Reykjavík. In 2000, Icelanders and Icelandic-Canadians commemorate two millennia: Leifur Eiríksson's arrival in Canada and Icelanders' conversion to Christianity 1,000 years ago. In 2001, Iceland and Canada will exchange embassies, ensuring the continuing cultural connections between these two northern neighbours.

I would like to express my gratitude to Arni Haraldsson for his support, openness, and generous spirit throughout the entire project. My thanks to James Patten, now at the Winnipeg Art Gallery, for his enthusiasm when I first proposed the exhibit, and to Brian Meehan for carrying forward this enthusiasm and providing guidance along the way. I would like to express my appreciation to Eleanor Bond, Susan Gibson Garvey, Jamelie Hassan, Patrick Mahon, Charlotte Townsend-Gault, and in particular Jennie White, Director of Educational Services, for their support and advice. Pauline Greenhill and Susan Schuppli have been wonderful editors, and I thank them both. Peter Smith has managed programming in conjunction with the exhibit. Bob Ballantine designed the catalogue, and Barry Fair handled the shipping of the work from Vancouver. Peter Hillborg and Scotty Hamer installed the exhibit. My thanks to all for making *At Last Sight* possible.

Dr. Anne Brydon
Professor of Anthropology, Wilfrid Laurier University

I WOULD LIKE TO THANK Anne Brydon for the interest she's shown in my work; Brian Meehan and Bob Ballantine for organizing the exhibition and catalogue. Thanks are due to Bill Boutin and Duc Le at ABC Photocolour, and also Brad Chernoff in Vancouver. I am grateful to Madhu Sarin for sharing with me her insights into Chandigarh; to Keith Wallace for the introduction to Ramanjit Singh and his family; to Judith and Moshe Mastai for putting me in touch with David and Tammy Adery in Jerusalem. Many are the friends and family across Iceland to whom I owe thanks; I am especially grateful to Guðmundur Oddur Magnússon, Guðrún Helgadóttir and Helgi Thorarensen for their assistance. Finally, to Lori Hinton for everything else.

Arni Haraldsson

foreword

THE LONDON REGIONAL ART AND HISTORICAL MUSEUMS is very pleased to be presenting this exhibition and publication of the work of Vancouver artist Arni Haraldsson. Haraldsson's extensive examination of the historical promise and contemporary reality of the modernist movement as expressed through the architecture of a number of the world's cultures has resulted in an impressive body of work.

Curator and essayist Anne Brydon is to be commended for not only bringing together this remarkable body of Haraldsson's work, but also for her catalogue essay which adds significantly to our understanding of Arni's work and some of the underpinnings of the dominant movement in twentieth century architecture.

The support of the City of London, the Ontario Arts Council, and the Canada Council for the Arts continues to be critical to the activities of the London Regional Art and Historical Museums as it allows us to bring this manner of exhibition programming to our museum public, and for this we are very grateful.

LRAHM staff are also to be commended for their efforts in bringing this project to realization. Bob Ballantine has once again designed a catalogue that beautifully complements the work on exhibition and Becky Boughner and Barry Fair have ably assisted in the organization of this project.

Most of all, thanks go to Arni Haraldsson for his generous cooperation in making this exhibition a reality. His assistance every step of the way has made this project a pleasure to be involved with and a significant accomplishment for LRAHM.

Brian Meehan
Executive Director

perfecting structure

Anne Brydon

WITH HIS PHOTOGRAPHS of cityscapes and mid-20th-century modernist architecture, Arni Haraldsson is focusing attention on the fragmentary remains of European modernism's extension into its borderlands. He seeks to show his viewers how the specificities of local life penetrate the built forms that embody the ideals of modernism. At the height of its influence, modernism had been a spare and geometric aesthetic, a utopian ideal for which societies could strive, a universalising strategy to establish social policies, and a practice of object-making ranging from chairs and poetry on the one hand to industrial agriculture and giant power dams on the other. Modernism hasn't left the world, although its hopefulness seems to have diminished. The traces of modernism remain around us, its project incomplete, its feet now more obviously made of clay.

The exhibit *At Last Sight* selects from three bodies of work that are part of a series of photo-documentary projects Haraldsson has completed since 1993 in and around Vancouver, as well as in France, Italy, South Africa, Israel, India, and his native Iceland. Both the exhibit and this essay are intended to prompt consideration of the artist's work as a practice of *critical nostalgia*, a self-conscious exploration of what he calls, using Walter Benjamin's phrase, the "just past." Haraldsson works in a deceptively simple way: his photos are portraits, only of buildings and places rather than people. He portrays structures that are too old to be considered new, but too new to be thought of as traditional or part of history. Their liminal status speaks to the gap between the post-war utopian ideals of modernism and the mundane and conflictual realities of contemporary urban life.

In India, Haraldsson examines the Capital Complex at Chandigarh, designed in the 1950s by the Swiss-French architect Le Corbusier and now the capital of the states of Haryana and Punjab. In Israel, the artist juxtaposes two cities: Tel Aviv, a planned city that began as a suburb of the Arab port Jaffa which rapidly expanded when Jews emigrated from Europe to there beginning in the late 19th century, and Jerusalem, an ancient city whose neighbourhoods and historical sites carry an overwhelming symbolic and political load. In Iceland, Haraldsson interweaves the sites of his personal memory in Reykjavík and the countryside with signs of Iceland's sudden and dramatic adaptation to the modernist project.

The title of this exhibit, *At Last Sight*, evokes an intuition of journeys and departures, of something slipping out of view and into memory, like a shoreline receding as the ship sets sail. Some writers have suggested that modernity is a state of mind obsessed with journeys and the passage of time. Evidence of this is to be found in the cityscapes that Haraldsson chooses to portray – the signs of people displaced by partition or war, historical sites memorialised while buildings fall derelict, a future anticipated with monumental concrete forms.

The traveller carries with her two images: one is the home left behind, the other the destination yet to come. She is in neither place, not in the past nor in the future. How, then does she experience the reality of the present, except perhaps as the residue of hopes and sorrows? In Haraldsson's art there seems to be a concern with the way in which our expectations, memories, and senses converge then diverge at the moment of perception. The image in the mind and the reality experienced through the senses only partly connect. The artist's dispassionate eye captures how people now dwell in modernity's incomplete project, adapting its geometries to the intimacies of their lives. Perhaps it is with these small gestures that we've come to occupy the present with a mingled sense of loss and longing.

the no place of modernity

It is debatable whether utopian visions are dangerous delusions and escapes from reality, or productive narratives and images that provide meaning and purpose to actions undertaken in their name. The idea of utopia (literally, "no place") is not new: inventing utopias has been the means for writers to criticise contemporary society since the time of Plato's *Republic* and St. Augustine's *City of God*. Thomas More's *Utopia* is the best known example, but the writings of Francis Bacon and Rabelais can also count as more earthly utopias. Jean-Jacques Rousseau's ideal of a primitive state of nature out of which humans have fallen influenced socialist idealists of the 19th century such as Saint-Simon, Fourier, and Proudhon. The means by which utopias could be achieved, however, were never clearly laid out. Utopia remained a place in the mind's eye until the technical capacities that mark the beginnings of modernity (arguably sometime in the 17th century) made earthly paradise seem buildable.

Nation-states are modernist social formations. The utopian ideal of a single people, united by origin (real or fictive), language or religious faith (or all three at once), forming a single polity within a clearly demarcated territory was literally revolutionary in the late 18th century. Revolutions in the United States in 1776 and France in 1789-91 set the tone for future political movements. Independent nationhood appeared as a solution to authoritarian monarchy, colonial oppression, economic stagnation, and social marginalisation to peoples throughout the world. New nation-states are still coming into being, and new nations are still dreamed into existence.

Iceland (1944), India (1947), and Israel (1948) became independent nation-states at the close of World War Two, part of a new wave of nationalisms sweeping across former colonies in Africa, Asia, Europe, and the Americas. In the post-war era, capitalism, industrialism, urbanisation, bureaucratisation, mass communication, individualism, science and rationalism – the canonical sociological categories through which modernity is understood – came together as powerfully transformative forces that drove nationalist movements. Nationalism's fixation on the forward movement of time set their achievement as a goal that could be materialised in the discourse and practices of modernisation and development. Instrumental rationality allied with capitalism and technology was assumed to improve the nation's citizens. The governments in Iceland, India, and Israel promoted modernisation projects, assuming that technology and rational planning could transcend the confusions and conflicts of volatile and desperate histories.

The dilemma and paradox of nationalism is precisely that rational progress relies on the very destruction of historical traces which define the authenticity of the nation. Nationalism valorizes the preservation of the past at the same time that it justifies its sacrifice to the inevitable forces of change. Nations become obsessed with historicity and primordialism, and some artists have tried to create a human dimension to modernity by reconfiguring at a symbolic level the bonds between people, history, and place. Consider how the Group of Seven achieved this for English Canadian nationalism by means of their landscape paintings.

But the alienating forces of urban living and the industrialised workplace, combined with the violence of nation-building that characterised India and Israel, generated a sense of dislocation and alienation that remain the unresolved experiences of modernism. It would seem that the tension between a nostalgia for what is lost and a desire for what is yet to come is how humans fill what Nadia Seremetakis calls the absence at the heart of modernity. Nostalgia she defines as an "unresolved historical experience", an attempt to fix the passage of time by holding onto a sensation (she describes her memories of eating a peach no longer grown in her native Greece) before it slips into oblivion. In the language of ethnicity, nostalgia is typically felt for the cohesiveness of farm or small town life, where belonging seems imaginable. In the last decade, nostalgia for modernist household objects and furniture of the 1920s through 60s has appeared amongst the under-forties. Is this the moment when modernism slips into the past, becomes understandable not as a lost ideal but as a category of collectible not so many years after its acknowledged failure?

Modernist architecture's appearance in the years following World War One grew out of and responded to that era's sense of dissolution and disorientation. The architectural historian William Curtis suggests that "this was the perfect ground for the growth of Utopianism tinged with an underlying *Angst*" (1996:183). The diagnosis of contemporary ills had been made by 19th- and early 20th-century social analysts such as Durkheim in *Suicide*, Freud in *Civilisation and Its Discontents*, and Marx in *Capital.*

In post-war Europe, some artists, writers, musicians, and architects – those charged with the creation of culture – turned to imagining material methods and forms to anchor people to deeper meanings as a counterbalance to alienation. They felt they carried the responsibility to provide modernity with a sense of humanity. Some architects thought it their task to realise the new, pluralist society by revealing its abstract forces through house plans and the layout of roads and districts. Others drew inspiration from machines such as the turbine, using its curvilinear shape or repetitive rhythm as a motif and in so doing aestheticising or spiritualising it.

The turbine shape appears in details of *Haus Aharanovitch 117 Rothschild Blvd (1934)*. The architect was a German

10. *(Skuld) Fate (1900-27) Sculpture Garden, The National Einar Jónsson Gallery, Reykjavík, 1997*

27. *Ceremonial Door, Legislative Assembly (1952-62) Chandigarh, Le Corbusier, architect/designer, 1996*

Jew who trained at the Bauhaus in Dessau, Germany. With others, he left Germany for Tel Aviv before 1933, the year that the Nazis closed the school because of its supposed subversion, decadence, and bolshevism. The house had once been on the most fashionable street, but now shows signs of fading in the coastal Mediterranean heat and humidity. The design features angular lines, flat roofs, and jutting balconies designed to cast sharp shadows in the direct southern light.

The sculptor Einar Jónsson was one of Iceland's first artists in the "high" cultural sense (wood carving, needlework, and church decoration had always existed in a country otherwise poor in workable materials). With a highly romantic visual language blending Icelandic medieval history and folklore with European theosophy and classical mythology, he created works of great emotionality. His sculptures *Sorg (Grief)* and *Skuld (Fate)*[1]

universalise and elevate human sorrow in a transcendent, redemptive spirit.

Similarly, Le Corbusier's *Ceremonial Door* assembles symbolic figures which the architect used to give visual form to his universalist philosophy. While the Open Hand – an odd blend of a Picasso peace dove with a giant Buddha's hand – is intended, as the insignia of the Chandigarh administration, to symbolise peace and reconciliation, the enamelled mural on the Legislative Assembly building indicates something of the architect's eclectic sources of inspiration. He symbolises an ancient solar cult (Egyptian?) and animal symbols (Indo-European? Native American?) that in his mind seem to have linked together as some pan-human symbolic foundation or cosmic law; similar icons and symbols are found throughout the complex cast in the concrete.

producing the image

Modernist designers tended to elide how things *looked* with how things *functioned*. Thus, rational social order in a city or farm was discernible by a visual aesthetic that favoured the regimented geometry of the grid. Such an assumption – that visual order equals social order – overvalues the visual as a source of truth. Photography as a mode of representation has underscored this conceit, in that it has been treated by the general public, who've made photography a familiar part of everyday life, as an unmediated access to reality. As an artistic practice, photography continually challenges the notion of objective reality. Its many techniques, aesthetics, and associated philosophies are relevant to understanding the deliberate choices Haraldsson makes in his work.

The image is and is not the reality: the literalness of his photos is a stylistic choice linked to the subject matter of modernism and architecture. Haraldsson uses several camera formats in his work. The 4 x 5, large format he uses for the landscapes and buildings: the camera requires time to position, and because the photographer must plan the composition by means of an inverted image in the viewfinder, it demands a deliberateness that works well with the genre of pictorialism. The 35mm, because of its more portable size and greater intimacy with the body's movement, renders the pedestrian's passage through the city with the apparent instantaneity of the snapshot.

The images which Haraldsson gives us are deliberately dispassionate and observational. He chooses to photograph in the diffuse brightness of light overcast days, to reduce colour saturation and the contrast of shadows that would otherwise heighten the images' emotionality. This approach is a deliberate aesthetic strategy which renders images shot

19. *Lifta, West Jerusalem*, 1997

26. *View of Capital Complex from Secretariat Roof, Chandigarh, India*, 1996

in different geographies in a similar light, thereby visually emphasizing the continuity between places that modernity sought to create throughout the world. When human figures appear in his photographs, they are incidental, more part of the landscape than forming a narrative through their captured actions. Haraldsson's photos are not dogmatic. In fact, it is difficult to know where he stands, figuratively speaking, in relation to his subject matter. One senses a creative ambivalence that allows space for viewers to form their own opinions.

Photographic technique thus emphasizes the issues of landscape, portraiture, and objectification that arise in relationship to modernist architecture and urban planning. In *Lifta, West Jerusalem*, Haraldsson uses the conventions of pictorialism and landscape art to produce an aesthetically pleasing cityscape. The same is true in *View of Capital Complex from Secretariat Roof*, yet both images are troubled once informed by a social reading. From the point of view of the former Arab neighbourhood of Lifta, Haraldsson is able to juxtapose that place to the Ramot Forests and the new Orthodox neighbourhood of Ramot. The juxtaposition highlights the geopolitics of Jerusalem's partitioning during the 1967 Six Day War. The Orthodox neighbourhood is transformed from the picturesque into a reminder of the political violence of the Jewish settlements. From the rooftop of the Secretariat in Chandigarh, a visitor similarly has a constructed vista (the roof had been intended as the location from which to admire the entire complex) that on closer

inspection reveals political violence. The soldiers and barbed wire have been in place and tourist access restricted since 1995 with the assassination of the Chief Minister of the Punjab, Beant Singh, in front of the Secretariat.

Both images use a raised point of view to create an ideal scene of apparent innocence that positions the viewer above and outside it. This is the touristic view, but also that of the outsider without the local knowledge to historicise the scene. Learning to read the landscape, then, becomes an act to subvert modernity's effacement of history as anything but the nation-state's myth of origin. These photos recall the aesthetic vistas of landscape painting, yet the residue of social conflict and abandonment to be found in them cannot easily be dismissed, thus complicating any nostalgia they invoke. The self-consciousness which informs Haraldsson's work produces a *critical* nostalgia, an awareness of how modernism constructs modes of looking at the environment. Typically, people don't view their surroundings as the manifestation of an idea or philosophy, or the result of historical choices. Instead, they see function and aesthetic in the most immediate and timeless way: is it comfortable? can I find my way around? is it beautiful? Haraldsson challenges this manner of benign looking and leads the viewer to consider what is happening in the landscape to make it appear timeless and naturally there, thus neutralised.

Chandigarh

Haraldsson described his impression of Chandigarh as a post-nuclear, post-apocalyptic city. The concrete already shows evidence of aging as the heat and humidity act upon it. The buildings seem intended to become future monumental ruins. The massive concrete structures of the Capital Complex – the Legislative Assembly, Secretariat, and High Court – are like large public sculptures, objects demanding to be viewed from particular vantage points. It's as if Le Corbusier anticipated the position of the camera in determining the stunning visuality of his designs. Von Moos calls them "monumental images of their content and function" (1977:431).

Chandigarh lies northwest of Delhi on the flat land of a river plain. It had been built as a capital for Punjab following Partition in 1947. By the 1880s, Indian nationalism had found expression in the battle for independence from British Rule. The British made a conciliatory gesture by allowing the establishment of the Indian National Congress in 1885. The domination of the congress by Hindus prompted the creation of the All-Indian Muslim League in 1906. In 1930, the idea of a separate Muslim state was first raised. The confrontational relations between the British Government, Congress and the Muslim League increased the intransigence and violence of both Hindus and Muslims to the point where Partition seemed to the British to be the only solution. When independence was granted by the British and the sub-continent partitioned in August 1947, the boundary cut through the predominantly Sikh state of Punjab. About five million Muslims left India for Pakistan, and about the same number of Hindus and Sikhs left for India. During the two-day, two-way exodus, about 500,000 people died in atrocities and another 12 million were left homeless.

In 1966, Indira Gandhi sought to reach a compromise with Sikhs wanting their own state of Khalistan, by partitioning Punjab into two states, Sikh Punjab and Hindu Haryana. Both states are governed from Chandigarh, which sits in Punjab on the border dividing them. This act did not satisfy extremists, who staged occupations of the Golden Temple at Amritsar during the 1980s and the 1995 assassination in front of the Secretariat building. In *Ramp, Secretariat (1952-58), Chandigarh*, Haraldsson emphasizes the weighty bulk of the building. The soldiers now permanently installed at the sight of the bomb blast killing Beant Singh and his assistants appear tiny and insignificant against its mammoth symmetry.

In the late 1940s, having lost their former capital Lahore to Pakistan, the Sikhs wanted a new capital city, preferably one built anew rather than another city taken for the purpose. India's first prime minister, Jawaharlal Nehru backed the project. At first, two architects from New York, Albert Mayer and Mathew Nowicki, were engaged to draw up plans for the new capital. After Nowicki was killed in a plane crash in 1950, Le Corbusier, aided by British architects Jane Drew and Maxwell Fry, took over.

28. *Ramp, Secretariat (1952-58) Chandigarh*, Le Corbusier, architect, 1996

25a, b. *Respiratory System* ... from *Corporal City*, 1996

30. *Samrat Yantra ... from Jantar Mantar (1725)New Delhi*, Jai Singh II, designer, 1996

29. *Entrance Hall, High Court (1952-56) Chandigarh*,
Le Corbusier, architect, 1996

For Le Corbusier, to be given the chance to realise an entire city *ex nihilo* culminated decades of ruminating upon the principles of urban design (his Plan Voisin of 1925 for the renewal of Paris by razing its core and constructing rows of rectangular skyscrapers was fortunately never undertaken). While much design work had already been accomplished, Le Corbusier set his stamp firmly on the final plans for the city and the Capital Complex. He altered the curvilinear streets laid out in the Garden City style by Nowicki, and replaced them with a rectilinear grid of thoroughfares. The city was structured with 29 sectors (numbered 1 through 30 since there was no number 13) measuring 800 by 1200 metres. Each sector was further subdivided into lettered sections. The sectors were grouped as either educational, commercial, industrial, recreational, or residential, following Le Corbusier's belief that all functions should be kept separate and distinct: visual order equals social order.

The layout adhered to Le Corbusier's Le Modulor theory that considered the city as a human body. Thus, the roads were the circulatory system, the commercial district its heart and its green spaces its lungs. In the photos *Respiratory System* and *Heart*, Haraldsson uses his 35 mm camera and smaller print size to convey the intimacy of the human body moving through the body of the city. The regular spacing of trees gives the green spaces a designed quality to them, transferring the regulated quality

of urban planning onto nature itself. This treatment of nature is echoed in the Geometric Mountain, a triangular wedge of a hill on the Capital Complex that is intended to refer to the nearby Shiwalik Hills, and is now used by patrolling soldiers as a raised viewing platform. The Capital Complex stands at the head of the body, at the north end in sector one. The various buildings of the complex were to be in harmonious relation with each other, based on the proportions of the human body, but lack of political will and money meant that not all buildings were undertaken.

The influences apparent in the Capital Complex are wide-ranging, but tend to be derived from other projects of similar magnificent proportions. There is something of Haussmann's Paris and L'Enfant's Washington in the layout of the boulevards and vistas. Lutyens' neo-classical design for New Delhi also influenced the architect in its proportions, as did the 18th century Moghul city of Jaipur, designed by its ruler, Jai Singh II. The latter's observatory, depicted in *Samrat Yantra*, is echoed in the rooftop of the Legislative Assembly. The scientific purpose of the original observatory is given an odd twist in Le Corbusier's obscure plans for an annual solar ritual to take place in one of the legislative chambers.

Construction was begun in 1952 in order to house 150,000 people. Later, sectors 31 to 47 were built, with a higher density to house 350,000 people, and now half-sectors numbered 48 through 61 are being built since the population has risen to about 850,000. As well, satellite cities also featuring the grid plan have sprung up in the region. As the city's population grows, it has little room to expand. Critics of Chandigarh have noted that the remarkable road system, replete with roundabouts and car parks, is out of place in a country where few people own cars and many get around on foot or by cycle- or auto-rickshaw. Sector 17, the heart, in particular, shows the signs of rapid decay, an ironic metaphor for an aging body. Unfinished apartment blocks are unbearably hot in summer without air conditioning. The open areas, vast expanses that make the city too difficult to get around comfortably by foot, are untended and the grass parched. In *View of Capital Complex from Secretariat Roof* the concrete open spaces between edifices are forbiddingly bare. The car park stands mostly empty.

Westerners have been quick to denounce the "unIndianness" of the city and the hubris of Le Corbusier's monumentalism. Fans of his architecture are divided on the success of this, his final work. Yet as Haraldsson found and others have also noted, the locals are quite proud to live in such a work of art, and those responsible for its expansion still adhere to guidelines sketched out by the architect. In his commentary on Chandigarh, von Moos notes that Le Corbusier's plan fit with the self-image and ideals of the Indian elite of the time, otherwise it would never have been built. Contrary to Gandhi's desire to oppose industrialism, Nehru embraced modernism, and saw India's future in large-scale industrialisation and building power dams. Technology, not ideology, was the ticket to prosperity, and Le Corbusier's designs gave expression to that utopian vision.

As I looked through a few tourist guide books on India to learn something of travellers' images of the country, I noted that in those books designed for those Westerners setting out to sacred India for purposes of spiritual tourism, Chandigarh is not mentioned. The "Indianness" they imagine and desire to experience can never be modern. The "unIndianness" criticism thus raises the question, who's image of India is the true one? Are Westerners giving vent to a nostalgia they project onto their Other? Or are the people of Chandigarh caught in an image of the future they still think can be achieved through Le Corbusier's geometric utopia?

Tel Aviv and Jerusalem

When tourists go to Israel they don't spend much time in Tel Aviv. It, too, is a new city, the economic and diplomatic centre of Israel, a cosmopolitan and, when compared to Jerusalem, a secular place. The lack of significant historical sites gives visitors no reason to linger. Only recently have the International Style edifices built during the 1930s and 40s attracted attention and restoration efforts.

Unlike other Mediterranean cities that grew more organically, Tel Aviv is laid out largely in a grid gone slightly awry, which unfortunately acts to block the cooling breezes from the sea. In the Neve Shanan district in Tel Aviv's south, streets are patterned in the form of the seven branches of a menorah. Inscribing of a significant symbol onto a place is not unique: in the older part of Reykjavík, streets such as Njálsgata and Bergþorsgata carry the names of people depicted in the 13th century Njálssaga, the finest work of the Icelandic saga tradition. The streets' placement in relation to one another mirror the interconnections between the characters. Even a city like Chandigarh, seemingly devoid of symbols, where streets and neighbourhoods have been assigned letters and numbers instead of names, becomes in itself symbolic of a desire for order, albeit a Western order.

Tel Aviv began as a garden city, loosely following the American urban planning philosophy championed by Ebenezer Howard as a solution to big-city congestion. Howard had been inspired by 19th-century utopianists like Robert Owen and Edward Bellamy, and his ideas such as zoning for use, bringing nature into the city, decentralisation, and green-belting have become standard practice throughout the world. For Jews leaving the congested ghettos of Europe, building anew with modern ideas must have been powerfully symbolic.

18. *138-42 Rothschild Blvd (1933) Tel Aviv, Israel,* Yehoshua (Shani) Steinbock, architect, 1997

Tel Aviv had been the first Zionist, all-Jewish city when it was established in 1909. It had begun as a small suburb of Jaffa, the Arab port and second largest city of Palestine. Until the latter half of the 19th century, Jaffa had been a city of Muslims and Christians. Over the millennia, it has been conquered at least 20 times: outsiders have sought its harbour and fresh water available from its many wells. Prior to the Jewish migration into it, the city prospered from its orange groves and silk production. The rise of Zionism and the search for a Jewish homeland (the British originally proposed Uganda as a possible site for it) brought Jews to the region who established the separate Jewish settlement of Tel Aviv, north of Jaffa. In 1917, the Ottomans expelled the Jews, but eight months later, when the British took control, they returned. In 1921, the anti-Jewish riots in Jaffa sent remaining Jews to Tel Aviv. Jews continued to leave Europe, many fleeing the rise of Nazism, others attracted by the Zionist nationalist movement.

16. *Model of Ancient Jerusalem II, Holyland Hotel, Jerusalem*, 1997

In May 1948 the creation of the State of Israel was declared from Independence House at #17 Blvd. Rothschild, blocks from the precise formalist example of Bauhaus architecture in *138-42 Rothschild Blvd (1933) Tel Aviv, Israel*. But the state of Israel's official line that Tel Aviv had been built upon unoccupied dunes denies the fact that, after the 1948 war, the city expanded over and obliterated four Palestinian villages. The UN partition plan for Israel proposed Jaffa as an Arab enclave in a Jewish state. Its population at the time was 100,000 people, but once the British withdrew, the Israelis surrounded all but one side of Jaffa and forced all but 4,000 of its inhabitants out. The state then settled Jewish immigrants in Palestinian homes, and over the last decades Jaffa has been gentrified for touristic consumption, erasing the signs of its former Arab status. Like the partition of India and Pakistan, the violence of state-making in

22. *Second Station* ... from *Via Dolorosa*, 1997

Israel has compounded Palestinian exile with the politics of Jewish Diaspora.

Jerusalem is the location for most of the sites sacred to Jews, Muslims, and Christians. The Western (Wailing) Wall is the most sacred for Jews; the Church of the Holy Sepulchre, the likely site of Jesus' crucifixion, is the most holy site for Christians; for Muslims, The Dome of the Rock, the place from which the Prophet ascended to heaven, is their 3rd most important site.

As a place of pilgrimage, Jerusalem is powerfully emotional. So powerful for those already deeply religious that, overwhelmed by the intensity of experiencing sacred sites juxtaposed to present-day political tensions, they succumb to Jerusalem Syndrome, wherein they believe themselves to be characters from the Bible. For Christians, pilgrimage involves recreating Jesus' path from Pilate's judgement hall to the site of the crucifixion, visiting each of the fourteen Stations of the Cross along the Via Dolorosa ("Way of Sorrow"). Crosses are available for rent. In *First Station*, soldiers, waste pipes, and a pop can are anachronistic reminders of both suppressed violence and 20th-century waste. *Second Station*, where Jesus took up the cross, is now a place where street hawkers sell their wares, and Palestinian graffiti declares " All…Should Be Set Free. The Twenty-seventh Memorial … The Democratic Front…"[2]

In *Model of Ancient Jerusalem II, Holyland Hotel, Jerusalem*, Haraldsson captures a curious consumable: a miniaturisation of the Second Temple, the city the Jews built in 515 BC, and of which only the Western Wall remains. Models give their audience an omniscient and controlling perspective; with this model the Second Temple has not been dedicated to Zeus by capturing Greeks (as it was around 195 BC), nor destroyed by Romans (as it was around 70 AD), nor crowded by tourists: it exists as a pure form, a perfect memory.

According to the UN Partition Plan, Jerusalem was to be a separate body, open to both Jewish and Arab states. Both sides vied for as much control of territory as possible before 1948, and neighbourhoods that had once been mixed became polarized. The city was formally divided between Israeli West and Arab East. During the 1967 war, Israel took over East Jerusalem and the Old City. Israel has declared it the single capital of the Jewish state, although few countries recognize this and maintain their embassies in Tel Aviv. Palestinians also consider Jerusalem to be their capital, and Arafat's current threat to unilaterally declare a Palestinian state can only exacerbate an already tense situation.

The question of Jerusalem remains the stumbling block to achievement of a Middle East peace deal. One commentator stated that for Jews, the issue is security while for Palestinians, it is honour. I would add redress and justice to that formula. The Pope wants to see the city run as an international endeavour, but the Jews, given the history of the Holocaust, are sceptical of the effectiveness and willingness of other governments to engage effectively in international governance. The intransigence over Jerusalem has increased over the last decades. Jerusalem has become an icon for all sides, increasingly central to identity and the personification of Palestinian-Israeli conflict.

Reykjavík

Reykjavík is a distinctly modernist city in a country that did not have towns or many villages before the 19th century. Farming with ocean fishing from open rowboats was the occupation of most Icelanders prior to the industrialisation of the fisheries around the turn of the 20th century. The city was not planned in the manner of Chandigarh or Tel Aviv, all of a piece, although by the 1920s plans for the city's development were being drawn up. Plans couldn't always keep pace with the demands of a growing population as people moved from the countryside and into the city.

Few buildings in Reykjavík date from before 1900. During the 19th century, when Iceland was still a colony of Denmark, traditional turf dwellings and a few stone cottages gave way to frame houses kit-built from Norwegian timber and clad, walls and roof, with corrugated iron. The unadorned iron was then painted in an array of colours: clear hues of white, green, light blue, red, grey, or umber lent a colourful if austere look to the treeless town with its unpaved streets. It's worth emphasizing just how small the country was at the time: in 1910, Iceland had only 85,183 people, of whom 11,600 resided in Reykjavík (compare that to December 1999, when the population of Reykjavík was 109,795, and the country's total population 278,702).

Early in the 20th century, concrete made from local resources replaced the more expensive imported wood, but was cast to imitate the *look* of frame houses. At first Scandinavian neo-classicism predominated in public buildings, but by the 1930s that style yielded to the functionalism then emergent from Germany. At this time, buildings were to adhere to a nationalist ethos that valorises the Icelandic language, medieval saga history and literature, and nature. This was achieved by imitating the layout of rooms found in the larger turf houses, or copying the pitch of their roofs and their exterior stylings, or surfacing the concrete walls with a dark grey mix of sand and ground sea shells, to mimic the colour of the sea, the sky, and the volcanic landscape. Another decorative element was derived from columnar basalt – a rock type found throughout the volcanically formed island. In *Reykjavík, Iceland*, these various styles appear together. In the left background, the National Theatre building features the columnar basalt motif. In *Grettisgata* and *Vatnsstigur*, Haraldsson details how streetscapes in the older downtown neighbourhood of Þingholt are characterised by juxtaposing styles from different eras.

Haraldsson examines the work of one architect in particular, Einar Sveinsson. Sveinsson was the first Icelandic architect to train in Germany; before him students had gone to Scandinavian countries for their education. He was one of the first architects in Iceland to herald the new functionalism, beginning around 1930. In 1934, the city appointed him its first city planner, responsible for the layout of neighbourhoods and the design of municipal buildings. As Ármannsson describes them, "his urban plans reveal a constant quest to harmonize the contrary viewpoints of 19th-century romantic concepts of planned squares and boulevards, and the functionalist notions of human values posited on the universal right to bright, healthy housing." (1995:44).

He rejected the nationalist styles of reproducing turf houses and using the columnar basalt motif. Instead, his designs are spare and geometric, expressions of an adherence to the qualities of the construction materials and the purpose of the edifice. Some features are adapted to the Icelandic environment, such as the low-hipped roofs and large windows for maximum light entry. The surfaces of his buildings are coated in ground

4.   *Grettisgata* ... from *Houses, Reykjavík*, Iceland, 1997

8. *Sauðarkrókur, North Iceland*, 1997

11. *Olafsfjörður, North Iceland*, 1997

minerals such as obsidian. The house, *Suðurgata 37 (1939) Reykjavík* is typical of his residential designs, with its balanced rectangular forms in the layout of windows and curving line on the window wall that echo the turbine lines of the houses in Tel Aviv. The curving lines appear as well on the balconies of *Hringbraut 37-47 (1942-44) Reykjavík*, an apartment block where Haraldsson's grandfather lived, and which had been Sveinsson's response to the mid-war housing shortage. The shallowness of the flats and arrangement of windows were designed to achieve bright rooms. In *Chinese Embassy, Viðimelur 27-29 (1945), Reykjavík*, one of Sveinsson's residential duplexes has been converted into an embassy. The red doors have a certain whimsy against the stark exterior, but the security camera adds a slightly jarring note. Its circular window, and the curved lines of the other buildings were part of Sveinsson's design vocabulary, stemming from a fascination with the purity and rationality of mathematics (Ármannsson 1995).

In *Assembly Hall, Melaskóli (1944-46) Reykjavík* the viewer can see the windows ornamented in a modernist style reminiscent of Le Corbusier's mural, giving an inspirational image of humanity. Below it is a map of Iceland, also to instruct children and guide them visually to imbibe the nation (I've noted that the map of Iceland appears with extraordinary frequency in all manner of locations in the country, a part of nationalist pride).

The curving lines in *Entry, Melaskóli (1944-46) Reykjavík* echo the rounded shape of the exterior, which in turn refers to the road encircling Melatorg, a (round) square from which roads exit like spokes on a wheel. The square was part of his overall neighbourhood design of houses and blocks of flats. When it was built, the school was thought such a beautiful building that it was used for city receptions and shown to visiting heads of state (Ármannsson 1995). The serenity of the entranceway in Haraldsson's photo belies the story I heard from a friend who'd attended the school in her childhood and had experienced the entranceway as the haunt for bullies. She recalls one fellow being hung by his belt from a coat hook and having to wait for a teacher to lift him down. The image of *Austurbæjarskóli (1924-30) Reykjavík* has a similar nostalgic mystery to it, with its diffuse light and arched hallway. Haraldsson attended this school as a child.

The relationship between the artist and the city alters in the series of photos made in Iceland. Haraldsson is not a tourist, nor is he in a strange land. Instead, he has returned to the places of his own memories dating from before he was ten years old. Reykjavík does not have any of the ethnic and religious conflict and violence that underscore the experiences of Tel Aviv, Jerusalem or Chandigarh. The displacements of modernity are peaceful here, and registered in his life with small details that nonetheless connect to larger forces at work in the world.

While Iceland's peaceful nationalist movement had been growing since the 1830s, the final referendum on independence from Denmark came in 1944, at the end of the war. Over 99% voted in favour. The wartime occupation of Iceland by British and American forces brought new roads, a cash economy, and Coca Cola. This injection of capital speeded up processes of economic change already occurring, since the fishing industry had provided the economic basis for independence. The Icelandic government, like Nehru in India, also counted on relatively large hydroelectric projects adding to the country's increasing prosperity. Today, cheap electricity is used to attract foreign-owned aluminium smelters.

In the 1960s, Haraldsson's father got a job in the north, and the family moved from Reykjavík, where he had been born, to Sauðarkrókur. In *Sauðarkrókur, North Iceland*, Haraldsson documents one of the coastal towns that in Iceland are a sign of modernity. Like other places, Sauðarkrókur has a dock and harbour facility. Post-war social planning policies sought to stem migration into Reykjavík with subsidies to support village harbours, trawlers, fishmeal and freezing plants. This slowed the movement but did not stop it. Fishing had been on the ascendancy since the century's turn, but the sheep and dairy farming that had once been the island's mainstay was growing reliant on subsidies. In *Ólafsfjörður, North Iceland* an abandoned farm house stands isolated in a valley, a sign of the rural depopulation that still continues as food imports replace what can be locally produced.

In 1968, the herring stocks around Iceland collapsed and the economy of the country was sent reeling, unemployment rose, and inflation skyrocketed. Although prosperity eventually returned, many young Icelanders emigrated to North America, Europe, or Australia. Haraldsson's family was part of that exodus.

falling into place

When the traveller arrives in the place to where she is going, she pauses to look around. This is what it feels like to be here, now, she thinks. Feet on the ground, head in the sky. It's just as she imagined it; it is nothing like that at all.

As an artist, Haraldsson has learned the languages of modernist photography and architecture, and has chosen how he wishes to relate to both. He shows his viewers how the constructed landscapes of modernity are full of meaning and moral implication. He does so with an admirable impartiality, a mixture of acceptance and gentle inquiry. On his travels to the sites he has chosen, he uses his cameras to frame the appearance of a place at the moment of his presence there. He has an idea of what he will see before he arrives, but the experience when his feet touch the ground is always something more. He has, like us all, been born into modernity and spent his life negotiating its consequences.

He is the traveller who returns to report on what he has seen. But returns to where? To home? Perhaps Haraldsson's photo projects are his process of defining what it means to come home when for many the idea seems fraught with contradictions. In his work he has not relinquished the idea or nostalgia for that bulwark against time's erosion which is modernity's project always to make it new. The deliberate beauty of his images shows his admiration for what they portray, without disguising imperfections. Haraldsson accomplishes his task with nuance, balancing loss and longing in the clarity of perception.

endnotes

1 "Skuld" actually translates as "debt", but at the Einar Jónsson Gallery and Sculpture Garden, where Haraldsson photographed this sculpture, it bore the English translation "fate." One can speculate that this translation for the foreign tourist raised the tone of the moral ambivalence associated with debt and poverty.

2 Arabic-to-English translation by Mohamed H. Amery.

bibliography

Ármannsson, Pétur H. 1995 *Einar Sveinsson, Arkitekt og húsameistari Reykjavíkur.* Reykjavík: Kjarvalsstaðir – Listasafn Reykjavíkur.

Curtis, William J.R. 1996 *Modern Architecture Since 1900.* London: Phaidon. 3rd edition.

Seremetakis, C. Nadia, ed. 1994 *The Senses Still.* Chicago: University of Chicago Press.

von Moos, Stanislaus 1977 "The Politics of the Open Hand". in *The Open Hand: Essays on Le Corbusier.* R. Walden, editor. Cambridge, Mass.: MIT Press. Pp. 412-457.

1. *Reykjavík, Iceland,* 1997

23. *Jewish Cemetery, East Jerusalem*, 1997

at last sight **27** Arni Haraldsson

list of works

ICELAND

1. *Reykjavík, Iceland*, 1997; c-print; 29x37" framed

2. *Assembly Hall, Melaskóli (1944-46) Reykjavík*, Einar Sveinsson and Ágúst Pálsson, architects, 1997; c-print; 29x33" framed

3. *Entry, Melaskóli (1944-46) Reykjavík*, Einar Sveinsson and Ágúst Pálsson, architects, 1997; c-print; 29x33" framed

4. *Grettisgata ... from Houses, Reykjavík*, Iceland, 1997; 8 c-prints; 24x30" each framed

5. *Vatnsstígur ... from Houses, Reykjavík*, Iceland, 1997; 8 c-prints; 24x30" each framed

6. *Chinese Embassy, Viðimelur 27-29 (1945) Reykjavík*, Einar Sveinsson, architect, 1997; c-print; 29x33" framed

7. *Suðurgata 37 (1939) Reykjavík*, Einar Sveinsson, architect, 1997; c-print; 29x33" framed

8. *Sauðarkrókur, North Iceland*, 1997; transmounted c-print; 50x60" framed

9. *(Sorg) Grief (1926-27) Sculpture Garden, The National Einar Jónsson Gallery, Reykjavík*, 1997; c-print; 24x28" framed

10. *(Skuld) Fate (1900-27) Sculpture Garden, The National Einar Jónsson Gallery, Reykjavík*, 1997; c-print; 24x28" framed

11. *Olafsfjörður, North Iceland*, 1997; transmounted c-print; 50x60" framed

12. *Hringbraut 37-47 (1942-44) Reykjavik*, Einar Sveinsson and Ágúst Pálsson, architects, 1997; transmounted c-print; 42x50" framed

13. *Austurbæjarskóli (1924-30) Reykjavík*, Sigurður Guðmundsson, architect, 1997; transmounted c-print; 50x42" framed

14. *Old Cemetery, Reykjavík*, 1997; transmounted c-print; 42x50" framed

ISRAEL

15. *Model of Ancient Jerusalem, Holyland Hotel, Jerusalem*, 1997; c-print; 24x28" framed

16. *Model of Ancient Jerusalem II, Holyland Hotel, Jerusalem*, 1997; c-print; 24x28" framed

17. *Haus Aharanovitch, 117 Rothschild Blvd (1934)* Itzchak Rapoport, architect ... from *Modern Apartment Buildings, Tel Aviv*, 1997; 8 c-prints; 29x33" each framed

18. *138-42 Rothschild Blvd (1933) Tel Aviv, Israel*, Yehoshua (Shani) Steinbock, architect, 1997; transmounted c-print; 42x50" framed

19. *Lifta, West Jerusalem*, 1997; transmounted c-print; 50x60" framed

20. *Untitled (interior) ... from Lifta*, 1997; 8 c-prints; 29x33" each framed

21. *First Station ... from Via Dolorosa*, 1997; 14 c-prints; 24x30" each framed

22. *Second Station ... from Via Dolorosa*, 1997; 14 c-prints; 24x30" each framed

23. *Jewish Cemetery, East Jerusalem*, 1997; c-print; 29x33" framed

INDIA

24. *Heart ... from Corporal City*, 1996; 8 diptychs direct prints; 37x29" each framed

25. *Respiratory System ... from Corporal City*, 1996; 8 diptychs direct prints; 37x29" each framed

26. *View of Capital Complex from Secretariat Roof, Chandigarh, India*, 1996; c-print; 29x33" framed

27. *Ceremonial Door, Legislative Assembly (1952-62) Chandigarh*, Le Corbusier, architect/designer, 1996; c-print; 33x29" framed

28. *Ramp, Secretariat (1952-58) Chandigarh*, Le Corbusier, architect, 1996; transmounted c-print; 50x42" framed

29. *Entrance Hall, High Court (1952-56) Chandigarh*, Le Corbusier, architect, 1996; transmounted c-print; 50x42" framed

30. *Samrat Yantra ... from Jantar Mantar (1725) New Delhi*, Jai Singh II, designer, 1996; 6 c-prints; 29x37" each framed

31. *Portico and Pool, Legislative Assembly (1952-62) Chandigarh, India*, Le Corbusier, architect, 1996; c-print; 27x32" framed

Arni Haraldsson

Born

Reykjavík, Iceland, 1958
Lives and works in Vancouver, Canada

Education

Master of Fine Arts, University of British Columbia, 1990
Diploma, Emily Carr College of Art and Design, 1983

Solo Exhibitions

2000   "Jerusalem", Catriona Jeffries Gallery, Vancouver

1999   Galleri Axel Morner, Stockholm (with Derek
       Root). brochure: Shep Steiner

       Trylowsky Gallery, Vancouver. brochure: Shep
       Steiner

1998   Catriona Jeffries Gallery, Vancouver

1995   Presentation House Gallery, North Vancouver.
       catalogue: Robert Kleyn, Arni Haraldsson

1990   Western Front Gallery, Vancouver

1989   Artspeak, Vancouver

1985   Western Front Gallery, Vancouver

1984   Or Gallery, Vancouver

Selected Group Exhibitions

2000   Utopiary, Burnaby Art Gallery

1999   Vertical Cities: Documenting Hong Kong and
       Vancouver, Charles H. Scott Gallery, Vancouver.
       catalogue: Trevor Boddy

       The New Spirit: Modern Architecture in Vancouver
       1938-1963, Vancouver Art Gallery

1998   Edge City: New Art from (& about) Suburbia,
       Surrey Art Gallery. catalogue: Christopher
       Brayshaw

1997   Road Movies, Portland Institute for Contemporary
       Art, Portland, Oregon

       On Iceland, Kjarvalsstaðir, Reykjavík, Iceland.
       catalogue: Hannes Lárusson

       Trade Routes: History and Geography, 2nd
       Johannesburg Biennale, Exhibition of International
       Contemporary Art.
       catalogue: Okwui Enwezor, et al.

1996   TOPOGRAPHIES: Aspects of Recent B.C. Art,
       Vancouver Art Gallery. catalogue: Grant Arnold,
       Monika Kin Gagnon, Doreen Jensen

1993   Beneath the Paving Stones, Charles H. Scott
       Gallery, Vancouver. catalogue: Robert Kleyn

1991   Van Seven Vancouver Artists, Wilkey Fine Arts,
       Seattle

1989   The Zone of Conventional Practice and Other
       Real Stories, Tour itinerary: Optica, Montréal;
       Galerie d'art de l'Université de Sherbrooke;
       Presentation House Gallery, North Vancouver; The
       Mendel Art Gallery, Saskatoon; The Toronto
       Photographer's Workshop/A Space, Toronto;
       Memorial University Art Gallery, St. John's.
       catalogue: Cheryl Simon, et al.

1988   In the Vernacular, Arts, Science and Technology
       Centre, Vancouver. brochure: Petra Watson

       Social Complex, Gallery Connexion, Fredericton,
       N.B. brochure: Michael Lawlor

1987   A Linear Narration: Post Phallocentrism, Optica,
       Montréal; Gallery 44, Toronto. brochure: Irene Dual

       Lost Vancouver, Urbanarium Festival '87, The
       Urbanarium Development Society, Vancouver

       Vancouver Artists' Bookworks, Artspeak,
       Vancouver

1986   Camera Works, Or Gallery, Vancouver

       Broken Muse, Vancouver Art Gallery. catalogue:
       Helga Pakasaar, Keith Wallace

1984   Pocorococo, Coquitlam Centre Mall, Coquitlam,
       B.C.

1983   October Show, Vancouver Artists' League,
       Vancouver. catalogue: Steve Harris, et al.

Selected Publications about the Artist

1999   "Arni Haraldsson – Catriona Jeffries Gallery",
       J.J. Lee, Canadian Art, spring

1999   "Edge City", Josephine Mills, Parachute No. 94

1998   "Report from Johannesburg: Mapping the
       Postcolonial", Eleanor Heartney, Art in America,
       June

1997   Svipmyndir frá Kanada", Lesbók Morgunblaðið,
       August

       "Interview", J.J. Lee, Trace, No. 1, UBC School of
       Architecture

1996   "Moving Ground Underfoot", Monika Kin Gagnon,
       catalogue essay, TOPOGRAPHIES: Aspects of
       Recent B.C. Art, Vancouver Art Gallery

1995   "Architecture and Photography", Robert Kleyn,
       catalogue essay, Arni Haraldsson: Projects on
       Vancouver Architecture and Landscape.
       Presentation House Gallery, North Vancouver

       "Arni Haraldsson – Presentation House Gallery",
       Eric Fiss, Parachute No. 79; Judith Mastai, C
       Magazine No. 46

1994   "Beneath the Paving Stones", James-Jason Lee,
       Parachute No. 74

1991   "Arni Haraldsson – Western Front Gallery", Phillip
       McCrum, Parachute No. 62; Petra Watson, C
       Magazine No. 28

       "Discovering the Defeatured Landscape", Scott
       Watson, Vancouver Anthology: The Institutional
       Politics of Art, edited by Stan Douglas, Talon Books,
       Vancouver

1990   "Telling Pictures, Revealing Histories", Bob Wilkie,
       Afterimage, April

1988 "Window Dressing", Peter Culley, Vanguard, April/May

1987 "Camera Work", Michael Lawlor, *Parachute* No. 47

"Broken Muse", Jane Young, *C Magazine* No. 13

"Vancouver Artists' Bookworks", Erich Ranfft, *Vanguard*, February/March

1987 "A Linear Narration: Post Phallocentrism", Earl Miller, *Parachute* No. 49

1984 "Third Hand", Merike Talve, *C Magazine* No. 3

Selected Publications by the Artist

1999 Artists' Project, "Modern Apartment Buildings, Tel Aviv", *Collapse* No. 4

"The Form of the City, The Face of the Social", in *So To Speak*, edited by Jean-Pierre Gilbert, et al., Art Textes Editions Prende Parole

"Le Corbusier's Unité d'Habitation, Firminy-Vert", with Lori Hinton, *On Site Review*, No. 2

1997 Artist's Project, "The Countersense of Chandigahr", *Daidalos* 64, "Rhetorics"

1994 Artist's Project, (Photographs and Text), *West Coast Line*, No. 15

1992 *Architecture as History: Ulrich Horndash*, catalogue essay, Contemporary Art Gallery, Vancouver

1989 "The Billboard as a Form of Public Address", catalogue essay *Transpositions - A Public Exhibition of Canadian Photography*, Active ARTIFACTS Cultural Association, SkyTrain Transit System, Vancouver

1987 "Tracing Collage, Montage and Appropriation", catalogue essay, *Transference*, Walter Phillips Gallery, Banff

Artist's Project, "Vertical Dreams", *C Magazine* No. 12

1986 "History at Infinity: Roy Arden", *C Magazine* No. 11

1985 "In-Quest of Folly: Reading Rodney Graham's *Lenz*", *C Magazine* No.5

1984 Artist's Project, *Impulse*, Fall

6. *Chinese Embassy, Viðimelur 27-29 (1945) Reykjavík, Einar Sveinsson, architect, 1997*

credits

at last sight: Arni Haraldsson

October 14 - December 3, 2000

London Regional Art and Historical Museums

Curator	**Dr. Anne Brydon**
Publication Design	**Robert Ballantine**
Preparation	**Scotty Hamer, Peter Hillborg**
Registration	**Barry Fair**
Administration	**Becky Boughner**

Cover: *Austurbæjarskóli (1924-30) Reykjavík*, Sigurður Guðmundsson, architect, 1997

We gratefully acknowledge the support of the Canada Council for the Arts,
the Ontario Arts Council and the City of London.

ISBN: 1-895800-84-6

London Regional Art and Historical Museums

421 Ridout Street North, London, Ontario, Canada N6A 5H4

(519)672-4580